KINGDOM OF GRAVITY

ACKNOWLEDGEMENTS

My gratitude extends to the following editors of the following publications where some of these poems, or versions of these poems, first appeared:

Resurrection Man (chapbook, Jai-Alai Books, 2017); *The Second Republic,* chapbook in *Seven New Generation African Poets* box set (University of Nebraska Press, 2014); "Resurrection Man", Red Bull Academy radio (2016); "The Shepherd", *The Golden Shovel Anthology* (University of Arkansas Press, 2017); "Prayer for Exiled Poets", *Read America(s)* (Locked Horn Press, 2015); "The Republic", *Poetry Review* (Winter 2012); "The Kingdom of Gravity", *Brittle Paper* (Summer 2016); "The Kingdom of Gravity", "At Gunpoint", "The Self" – Winner of Brunel African Poetry Prize 2015; "At Gunpoint", "The Devil's Clothes", *Callaloo* Vol 39 no 3 (2016); "The Dark", *Liberation Anthology* (Beacon Press) (2015), *Aesthetica Creative Writing Anthology* (2016 Edition), and *Mamga 62* (Summer 2015); "Deathfall", *New Boots and Pantisocracies Anthology* (October 2016); "Deathfall", "The Light That Found Its Voice", *Wasafiri* (Winter 2016); "Candidate A", "The Informer", *One Throne Magazine* (Summer 2015); "Ugandan Golgotha", "Smoke", *Cordite Review* (Summer 2016); "LHR", third place in Babishai Poetry Competition 2015; "A Crocodile Eats the Sun", *In Protest Anthology* (Human Rights Consortium U.O.L, 2013); "How A City Vanishes", "How To Make Blood", *Rialto 81* (Summer 2014); "Stone", shortlisted for 2010 Arvon International poetry prize and in anthology; "From the King", shortlisted for 2010 Troubadour poetry prize; "Citizen", *South Bank Poetry Magazine* (2012); "Beatitude", *Being Human* (Bloodaxe, 2011); "The Last Ugandan", *Journeys Home* (African World Press, 2009); Beatitude", "Prayers for exiled poets", "Father Cornelius", *Ten Anthology* (Bloodaxe, 2010); "The Republic", Newham Writer in Residence Commission, Spread the Word 2010.

NICK MAKOHA

KINGDOM OF GRAVITY

PEEPAL TREE

First published in Great Britain in 2017
Peepal Tree Press Ltd
17 King's Avenue
Leeds LS6 1QS
UK

Printed & bound by Imprintdigital.com, UK

ISBN 13: 9781845233334

Supported using public funding by
ARTS COUNCIL
ENGLAND

Hold mud in your hand
gathered from the city you live in.

Knead it like cassava in your palm.

Add white light from the sky
and coal dust from beneath the soil.

This book is for my wife, daughter and son – My kingdom

How can I turn from Africa and live? – Derek Walcott

CONTENTS

MBA

Minutes after the airbus took off, a German girl in 1st class
starts talking about the afterlife and things that belong to the dead.

One man swallows duty-free rum to replace the taste of sugarcane,
his skin hissing and spitting like a fuse as the sun glides in reverse.

He is mastering the art of being a very persistent illusion.
This is mine; *the world is connected by a circle.*

*The same circle a man might make folding his arms around
another man's shoulder.* Light bends through the cabin.

At the edge of my window small towns pass.
Clouds cascade and dance.

We are both holding our breath, reciting the laws of probability.
My eyes are closed. I call it the garden of the blind.

I am back in the old world where light bends through the clouds.
The soldier by the kiosk loves the taste of his words.

Women jostle for provisions. Their children wade ankle deep
in water. Their reflections dance across the surface.

Two continents away a cameraman lifts his hand for silence
in the oil refinery that looks bigger than he imagined.

Two men walk in the dark. The camera lens searching
for the quality of lost light. They are moving by memory

of a stolen blueprint tattooed on their minds.
I have the same tattoo.

HIGHLIFE

Presidency can buy you celebrity.
Wrap your hand around
the right man's throat

and you can become a member
of the elite. Watch
the shape of a man

in your palms as he longs
for old places.
Offer him breath

in exchange for all he has.
From your feet he will see the world
differently. When he prays,

he will know that you are God.

BIG NATION

He promises us that there will be much to eat
after the shootings. That they'll order all the "finest".
We bow, as is custom for elders in our river village,
faces turned, eyes closed. Some don't buy the talk.

But the sky is smoking at the edge of town where the plane
fell. Soldiers return bloodbathed as the crowd
builds; they speak in clicks. An empty stomach growls.
I must have drifted to a far-off sound. Big names gather.

Some have camped on the path – middle-aged folk,
children born with phantom limbs, a shaman
(with a painted tooth squatting over burnt ash),
a girl playing hopscotch with a child slumped over her shoulder.

The albino dog looks up at me. I squat. His tail wags
mosquitoes off my shins. And when he asks, I tell him.
This man is a firm knot in our chest. A landlord draped
in Savile Row suits, who uses our towns as a race track.

Mark the length of his shadow; where it reaches,
men fall. What can he buy with food that was
not ours already? What god is he? No moon and star fear him.
He is not of our blood.

We were once many before the imperials, before our nation
changed hands, before the world called it a nation.
What wind is he that I must kneel like a man in prayer?
Why must I whisper? He is not my flag.

KING OF MYTH

Back when you were taken from our lives like
the son of God ascending into heaven at the barricade
to another life, policemen on their motorbikes
named you King of Myth. You danced to tossed grenades,
all part of the charade in their fire ritual. In a restless air
we surrendered our weapons – axe heads, shanks, short rope,
blades, some poison and all its animal understanding – now fair
game to the enemy with our world in their scope.
They came down hills during the blackout, phantoms
from a fallen sky with years of practice at soft landings
onto roofs in darkness, like a spirit slipping into skin.
The voice of their guns kept the violence from escaping.
A disturbance in the trees is easily mistaken for wind.
Honey I'm still free, take a chance on me – as the radio sings.

BEATITUDE

When a rebel leader promises you the world seen in commercials,
he will hold a shotgun to the radio announcer's mouth,
and use a quilt of bristling static to muffle the tears.

When the bodies disappear, discarded like the husk of mangos,
he will weep with you in those hours of reckoning and judgement,
into the hollow night when the crowds disperse.

When by paraffin light his whiskey breath tells you
your mother's wailings in your father's bed are a song
for our nation, as he sits with you on the veranda to witness a sunrise,

say nothing. Slaughter your herd. Feed the soldiers
who looted your mills and factories. Let them dance
in your garden while an old man watches.

Then when they sleep and your blood turns to kerosene,
find your mother gathering water at the well to stave off
the burning. Shave her head with a razor from the kiosk.

When the fury has gathered, take her hand and run
past the fields' odour of blood and bones. Past the checkpoint,
past the swamp towards the smoky disc flaring on the horizon.

Run till your knuckles become as white as handkerchiefs.
Run into the night's fluorescent silence. Run till your lungs
become a furnace of flames. Run past the border.

Run till you no longer see yourself in other men's eyes.
Run past sleep, past darkness visible.
Stop when you find a country where they do not know your name.

STONE

The best thing I did was
    move my body from one side of the world
to the other. This required a visa,
    which required a bribe.

The bribe, placed in the palm
    of a man with a gun,
took my mother's monthly wage packet.
    The man with a gun

let you speak to a clerk.
    He too wanted a wage
because it would be his job
    to have words with a judge

for another month's salary.
    The official wanted his bribe
so listened to the clerk
    escorted by the soldier as he held his gun.

As I sat with my mother
    at the steps of the court,
drinking soda, waiting
    for one man to say yes, my mother said,

"In Uganda, a bribe stops men
    doing nothing. It rolls away the stone."
Her sips were slower than mine,
    each separated by this prayer.

COMRADE

Comrade! Take the fire, its marrow and ash.
Take what vanishes and now repeat.

Without risk take the nation, its boundary.
If it miscarries take the calves and now repeat.

Take the soul and its vigour – make us vagabond.
Take the women and their fruit and now repeat.

Take the musician's tambourine and tilt of hip,
the wisdom a body forgets in motion and now repeat.

Take this world, its reflection, my memory of it,
place it in the boot of your car and now repeat.

Take the mountains, their wind and silence,
their gram and ounce and now repeat.

Take the tomb, its sharp edge and warriors,
all their bloody exhaustion and now repeat.

Take the future's and her search for freedom,
for an alias along the wall of time and now repeat.

Take our sleep as it narrows and what it drinks,
ourselves losing ourselves and now repeat.

THE REPUBLIC

In 1979, when the world ends,
there will be guns, AK-47s spitting
like mechanical dragonflies into a Kampala night.

There will be militia, who use barbed wire
to hang men by their genitals
from the arms of trees like cows.

There will be melted corpses chewed
by hyenas at the roadside; even the stench
of urine will not curb their hunger.

The price of beer
will be cheaper than a loaf of bread
now that the Asians have gone.

Blood loosened by machete blades
will flow down the Kisigi Hills
to the throat of Lake Victoria.

No longer will we fall
at Amin's feet as if dead,
even while the hills burn.

THE BEE

When the sun abandoned me,
the sky was an iris of black glass.
Nights kept me sleepless;

the trick was to unblink
the eyes till morning,
whether open or closed.

Butterflies in the tall grass
taught me to cling
to the world's back.

As my mind swung in on itself,
I could hear the river stretch
towards the stones.

The thought of death set fire to dreams.
In the shapeless dark, I pieced enough together
to see trees ghosting themselves.

They stood around a dead man
who had been stung
by the invisible bee of my bullet.

This edge of the world
was close to the border.
Like lightning behind a bank of clouds,

I hid from this scene.
It could have been worse.
He could have shot me.

A VIEW OF KIDEPO VALLEY

The wounded have forgotten their words.
At this hour the earth slows down.

Where their feet once walked my eyes now go;
it is an old-fashioned dance, like the tango.

To the fate of a note, they have matched this motion of battle.
The last thing they will remember are ants at their ankles.

That's not a man in pain, it's his body wrestling with the earth.
A bullet to the lung has dislodged his soul to the dirt.

Blisters and punctures are what's left of the body.
Dead goats in the field know this equality.

Tyrants have shown their hand.
These corpses will want their revenge.

From the clays of the body, blood now blossoms.
The ruins of our land have become your museums.

A CROCODILE EATS THE SUN

The stones on the riverbank have seen you.
Among the tepid reeds, you drink the night.

A lozenge of moon rests in your throat,
thirst for flesh sweeter than dik-dik fermenting in the gut.

Your nostrils peer through the lake to reveal
the curve of the earth as the world is split in two.

A praying mantis skating along blue mud
knows your secret. Even the bullet lodged

in your right eye cannot persuade you to stay
by the boundary. Stones are silent.

A weeping willow has its back turned. The rope
around its waist anchors a wooden boat to shore.

Beside dogtooth violets, a soldier's face is reflected
in the rippling glass. A standing portrait ready for war.

You were Idi Amin's teacher? He learned to wrestle
with you in the swamp during the cruel months?

In the shadow of night, with your bodies oiled in mud,
you got a taste for dying, decay and carnage?

Wrath the only nature of God you taught him.
What of mercy, peace and Uganda?

Our bodies still rest in your jaws.

PRAYERS FOR EXILED POETS

Were you to ask me where I've been...
I would have to tell how dirt mottles rocks.
How the river, running, runs out of itself.
　　　　　　　— Pablo Neruda, "There is No Forgetting (Sonata)"
　　　　　　　　　　　　　translated by Forrest Gander

Prayers no longer hold up these walls in my absence.
My own country rebukes me. I hold the world on my back.

Look for me in translation. In my own language you will go unanswered.
My Ugandan passports are a quiet place of ruin.

Where I come from, money is water slipping through their hands.
They eat what falls from the trees and turns the flesh to gin.

I am of the same fruit and close to extinction.
My only root is my father's name. Both of us removed from the soil.

In recent times, despite my deeds, you let me stay
no longer in bondage between earth and sky. No longer

do I hide in my own shadow. No longer waiting to stop waiting.
This rock becomes a sanctuary from which I can repair the ruins.

You have given me back my eyes.

EBB:

Entebbe International, the guards have rifles.
Their fatigues are tucked into black leather boots.
Milky-yellow teeth smile as they suck on sugar cane,
spitting the pulp on to the tarmac. My passport
has expired. One soldier hangs a transistor radio
on his bayonet as he barters with the kiosk attendant for

20 Malboro blend 28. Flamingos perch on the edge of Lake
Victoria – the way I have seen men perch at the river Ganges.
I'm wearing cream chinos and a denim sky-blue shirt.
My caramel Timberlands match my leather wristwatch.
And the radio says this is the closest you will get to be
Harrison Ford in *The Raiders of the Lost Ark*. I haven't
watched the film since then. I find it hard not being a hero.

RESURRECTION MAN

Somewhere west of our sacred sites, the ghost
of your former self is rising from captivity.
Your student friend, the one who saw you last,
swears she left you alive in the taxi. Even after my
two-fisted punches. She denies being the one who
gave the signal for dark men to change their shapes
in the night as you knelt, blindfolded. I want to believe
she had no part in the shaving of your hair and pubic mound
in front of onlookers. Rebels kneading your breast
like posho in their palms, begging in turn for your body,
bleached by their jeeps' headlights. Once broken,
you were dragged by the arms across the grass
onto the unpaved taxiway of Arua airport. Then
one yelled, "Burn her! The witch." Their echoes agreed.

One lit the match, another peeled the blindfold,
the rest poured gin on your face. I know you saw me
in the hollow of a tree. I wanted to run to you
but their bullets would have easily caught up with me.
I stood firm, learning to hide myself in the dark.
A man must have two faces: one he can live with
and one he will die with. The second face is mine.

THE SECOND REPUBLIC

When the hills were on fire,
there were no angels to guide us.

Only the equator was able to divide
the land equally. Even the night took sides.

If you were wise you found a body to cling to,
bosoms to rest your shoulders against,

something to be violent with and crave like salt.
Those caught in the fields never made morning,

bodies torn from their heads and left to cook
in the heat of a new day. I knew then it would take

time to remove the fire from the landscape,
slim flames cracking like whips under heaven,

brushing against our faces, charring the rooftops,
glistening in the ruins. Burning through the soles of my feet.

AT GUNPOINT

My body is the protagonist watched by soldiers
in patrol cars. Roof down, the front windscreen
frames them. Amin's voice bleeds
from a radio wafting up into a window of sky.

The *Times* will report of people
being forced to volunteer to avoid
being a body hiding in a toilet
or a corpse folded on a table.

I have heard men say *We will serve you.*
Others will say he saved them,
and yet others will flee, by passage
out to a border that no longer exists.

I have only made it as far as the long grass,
virgin territories whose mountain plains
and tribal inhabitants are a garnish,
part of a failed colonial experiment.

Holding my breath, words are now shadows
walking me down a corridor of all the wrong things
that brought me here. In this cracked republic
I have made a film of my life and played myself.

A man can't but look into his own imagination
to solve the conflict of himself. *Should I have been
the doctor, or a poacher in the clearing, a mad man,
or shepherd boys minding their business?*

All soldiers must die – some by bullet, some by knife;
the sharpest cut is betrayal. Lips are their usual servants.
I do not want to know the whistle of a bullet in the air
or how it seeks blood to release the weight of the soul.

DON'T WALK IN FRONT OF ME, I MAY NOT FOLLOW – CAMUS

A man on the bus turns to me
and says, *The rebels are observing you.*
Cars blur past, their headlights white as charcoal.
The driver swerves in the turning lane.
The rearview mirror loses sight of me
as I alight and slip into a bar. I dance, I drink.

He follows not to kill me but wrap
his arm around my waist.
He smokes fire into the oven of his throat,
exploring my flesh with his fingertips.
The blood in his erection undisguised,
I give him my eyes, now seashells,

the word I use to describe everything else,
a land neither of us recognise.
I forget everything but myself and your name.
When I say me, you hear an ocean inside you ascending,
but the air moves; it must know something you don't.

Dear Navigator, bless the high places.
You who saw the world's rapture in my eye
and did not blink. You who spoke to God
without doubting. Who came from the mountain
with tablets of dirt. Who slept with angels
and threw their names into the sulphur lake.
You who told the moon it had found a mate
and kept her waiting.

I lift up my eyes to the hills and there is God
sitting on a curb fuelled with bourbon.
Cigarette-paper skin melts off the body.
A path of ants eat his takeaway. A gift
Ah shit! Some smiles act like heat shields
for re-entry to reality.

THE DARK

You will try to make sense of the terrain, its limits on reality,
its secondary sounds – the crickets speaking pure rhetoric.

What is the year? No matter. Stripped of remembrance,
isn't the dark a grave, an axis by which all are measured,

the final mountain? Blessed are the dead whose bodies
are buried in the bosom of the earth. Blessed are those

who no longer taste fury, who, when brought to silence,
make dust their paper. In these hours of damp

the sky will witness bombs, hollow out our city. Be vigilant,
choose your executioners well, do not talk of wills.

Bless the pavements that will become your burial grounds,
for what can we give except our bodies?

Those who were your children will make homes in doorways.
Cover your heads; our patriarchs have been ripped off walls.

It's not the dark but what it leaves behind. A servant girl on her knees
gives testimony that the king has been added to our day's dead.

Lose respect, lose ceremony, lose duty, lose circumstantial
evidence, lose the code – my father should not have died today –

lose the law, lose remembering, lose absence. In the absence
of the law, truth will not be written down. Lose those who break it –

cowards who confess on scratchy radio broadcasts, field-generals
and their informers. Lose epitaphs. I have my father's eyes

and ratchet smile. Mirrors betray me. What anchors
me has drifted to the boundary. What a poor murder. He should

have died at war – close combat, an instep to the shoulder, then a knee
to the chest. Or his crown caught in the scope of a Simba rebel's eye

as the world draws close. Not caught off guard in a drunken brawl
over his wife. This is not how the loss of light should come to the world.

THE DEVIL'S CLOTHES (CURFEW JANUARY 1971)

Didn't we make you president to remove us
from the elsewhere? *I'll get us back our city*.
Isn't that what you said

perched on top of your jeep, when the troops
told you that we were sick of eating grass?
My village gathered songs on a sleepy Kampala road

to rest them at your feet, our hopes rising
bread, but it was the bodies that you wanted.
This time it wasn't the earth that cried blood.

We too would have been missing men if we stayed.
So we escaped like water from a cracked gourd,
while our wives let you wear them as hides.

If I had been born as flint
or glass, I could have ripped off their second skin.
Who would have blamed me on that cruel night?

Its darkness is tattooed on my eyes. An evening
that slips back into my mind as memories seize
and sting, where nothing leads you into nothing.

THE KINGDOM OF GRAVITY

We are not Alexander, who conquered worlds
giving them new tongues, but we share the story
of a ship resting on an African river, unbuckling
at its shore, awakened by the night's cold hard rain,
staring at the face of the Nile as it reminds you

> *You are a hawk*
> *silent in the voice*
> *of a midnight universe.*

What makes a man name a city after himself,
asking bricks to be bones, asking the wind
to breathe like the lungs of the night,
asking the night to come closer, to speak
to you as a tribe, asking the tribe to sleep,
asking sleep to loosen its language, asking
language to dream? Come close to me.

Can you not see that I am in search of fire,
the unshapen song of light? In my mouth
is a name hovering like smoke, spoken to me
by the oracle. Like others, I was in search
of a forest, a place to call home.

But what can I tell you about Kingdom,
about having the world at your feet?
When you have seen all the earth's boundaries,
you will crave for mirrors, searching for them in streams,
and when the river looks back at you
how will you be sure that nothing is lost?

THE INFORMER

So much depends on how the day starts. A closed sign
in the window, a train passing, the exchange of notes,
clouds not fully formed turning red, a young man
describing a ghost. The fear of the invisible shapes itself:
contours of his father's face in front of the city with no roads,
people living in tents, coarse dust under their feet,
a permanent apparition as children act out a war
by the corrugated kiosk. His fingers are a pistol grip.
He wishes for sleep but the body walks (his father listening)
towards an empty car lot in the day's fever. What better way
to camouflage himself than in the embrace of a civilian,
their voices a badly dubbed Chinese film punctuated
by kisses in the back of a pick-up truck. Later tonight
a live satellite feed will tell us a nation has changed hands.

HOW TO MAKE BLOOD

From the hands of boys with guns.
From angry men who chain-smoke.

From the land and its location
(a town of little charm).

From merchants now retired for years.
Sailors working as collaborators

in thankless jobs. Shipowners with crucial
information whose pay is minimal.

Traders hiding in an everyman appearance,
part invisible, well placed to be informers.

Wage earners who, in marked cars,
planned the ambush of the minister's

daughter's school bus while still in motion.
Slaves not mentioned by name but by clan,

trained to watch the troops on dawn raids.
If you ask around they'll tell you; they saw

the journalist walking past slim trees,
past the fruit kiosk, past the bicycle stand

through the main thoroughfare, past
the market, hypnotized by street hawkers

selling metal figurines, past the radio powered by
an exposed car battery hanging from a branch,

the radio's voice mouthed by the journalist,
past the crowd, who move as one body.

The song disturbed by helicopter blades
on the horizon. She shifts; under the skin

a muscle in the neck moves, shows electric
understanding. A change again, the pilot

has her in his sights. Clenched jaws
give the face distinction.

With the eyes of suns, a boy watches
her turn her finger into a gun.

HOW A CITY VANISHES

All it takes is two men on a bike,
a convoy in their rearview mirror,
some land, a shortage of visas,
the closing of embassies, a night
lowering its curtain of curfew
and some C-4 to turn a dirt highway
into a makeshift airstrip.

Out come the men in uniform
following the flare of a flashlight
towards life lurking in the long grass.
White soldiers, with foreign words
that taste too much like caution,
huddled around a wireless waiting
for orders, keeping their voices down.

A war reporter, tourist and volunteer
with the same faces just cleared
a checkpoint. Said they were on safari,
hence the cameras. Tonight they will make
the weekend edition of *People*. Tomorrow
our city, or some version of it, will be as
familiar as the dark side of the moon.

NBO:

Jomo Kenyatta International Airport.
Flight SV 446 from Jeddah delayed by
18 minutes. We are stuck in a holding pattern.
The hostess is collecting headphones and the pilot
has engaged the landing gear. The man next
to me has spent the whole flight pacing the aisle,
rolling Dhikr beads with his right hand. I pick up
his copy of *Vanity Fair*, August issue, with naked
Demi Moore pregnant with her daughter, Scout.
Her whole body is covered in permanent black marker.
Demi says I should read the book, *Song of Lawino*.
The man is holding his beard and calling God's name.

WATCHMEN

*This alone, I was convinced, had driven him out to the edge of
the forest, to the bush, towards the gleam of fires, the throb of
drums, the drone of weird incantations…*
— Joseph Conrad, *Heart of Darkness*

An outboard Yamaha engine got me this far.
I was in two minds: return or paddle for the contraband alone.
This for a saggy-breasted wife and two swollen children.
I would trade a month's salary and staples for a beer and a malaya.
Was that the marker (a blue buoy)?

I'm reeling in weighted jerry cans full of antibiotics, rice, oil and salt
and I'm convinced a man is on the water,
between me and the riverbank. He has in his right hand a lyre.
The melody has driven them out —
soldiers covered in cement dust and a party of shepherds.
How does the Nile hold him?
The apparition that cheats my eyes sings out:

> *Have you heard the sigh of a monarch in exile Ah Ah Ah!*
> *To you I say the limbs are mine*
> *his heart is mine and the knife is mine Ah Ah Ah!*

Some soldiers at the edge of the assembly
accept this as a sign from the gods.
Thirst climbs up my throat. Is this part of the enchantment?
Then the one who Gaddafi knew walks to the verge of the forest,
rips off his fatigues with the joy of a mad man to expose his breast,
picks up a sheep in the soft grass and tears it apart by the ribs.
Then pointing to the bush he says,

> *You who are not circumcised do not greet me.*
> *Head towards your mother's bosom. To you who are my*
> *true bloods, share the heart and thigh.*

By now all the herders and huntsmen have a gleam in their eyes
and have stripped down. All their sighs are of victory.
I am one of them, my hand carrying coals to set up fires.
We drink for our grandfathers who have gone below,
wearing the gin's heat like a coat.
Men are passing around the heart as it throbs.

Those who could see better than hear,
read too much into the gesture.
Some of them let off a few rounds,
using whatever their palms and feet could find as drums.
Some say he had promised land, others positions,
and yet others gold. The truth is we all wanted
to be kings with wives and cars.
There is a drone in our voices.

The night's coolness has not yet gone.
The apparition snatches a Kalashnikov from a shepherd's fist
and slips into the river. What's weird is we all break rank
and like a swarm follow singing his incantations
and like a swarm follow singing his incantations.

UGANDAN GOLGOTHA

1.

The rebel is all shield and sword.
You are all flesh and feet,
already dead in this old Europe.
A road of neon dirt grows
towards a checkpoint.
An Acholi soldier laughs
in hyena soliloquy.
Blood and wine from hills
are filled with dying. *Nixon
knew about Africa's problem.*

2.

Acacia trees whisper and disappear.
A moonless night hides its face.
The line of you does not move,
cautious of how time and light
can be a revelation. You move
towards a twilight away from the city
that is no longer home or hiding place.
The blood of one man against a soldier,
against a clan, against the caravan of men,
against the flash of fire, against teeth and tongue.

CANDIDATE A

For the record, he loves his own reflection,
this farmer's son from the delta. A splendid type.

Bone from the neck up, trained in wickedness,
born to lead, useful against the Mau Mau.

Unprovoked, he once cracked a cow's skull
with flat palms as the beast stared at him.

Did the same to three cattle-herders at Lake Turkana.
Reached into their necks to eat their intestines (allegedly).

He should have been court-martialled,
especially after the assassination attempt.

Such men rise in the ranks and can only be removed
by death or revolt. I suggest we seduce him with wives.

Surround him with ceremony, regulation and rules
even though secretly he feels they do not apply to him.

Feed him with titles: His Excellency, Field Marshall,
Effendi etcetera. His cravings have no limit.

We can use distrust of competition to our advantage.
He will demand acclaim in an unbridled urge to destroy.

Easily compensated, he does not accumulate goods
or possessions for the future, opting for immediate gratification.

While he buys friends, kills citizens without fear of god or religion,
in his effort to be remembered, we will make our mark.

KILLING CRAFT

Boy in army fatigues has his palm
on a gun. Boy smokes ganja,
says it makes him run.

Boy has the same name as me,
from the same clan. Boy killed his father
and buried him in the sand.

Boy leads a battalion but can't spell
his name. Boy has river of AIDS
running through his veins.

Boy sleeps with twelve virgins
to make it disappear. Bet you boy
will be Abraham by the end of the year!

Boy thinks he's Chuck Norris,
thinks he's Bruce Lee. Boy learned
Krav Maga in training camp led by Israelis.

Boy uses freight trains to disguise
his advance. From behind, boy
asks Nasiche for a dance.

Boy's back teeth as sharp
as bayonets. Sucks her breast
with war-gin breath.

Boy knows her bride price
will fall, she spread-eagled
with her back up off the wall.

Boy's eyes are a moon-white
stare. Inside her body
he goes off like a flare.

Looks down the street, his troop
in a jeep. Gives the bird.
It's time to retreat.

BOOK OF THE DEAD

To you the already dead, to those dying
in their sleep, to those flooded by a wet
season that did not wait for next year's crop.

To the weeping, the wounded. To those hiding
in the fever of a night waist-deep in mud.
To those standing in line for the body of Christ.

To the smoke, the only thing that rises
without interrogation. To the thirst left
in the mouths of men, quenched by the glass
of a woman, the glass of another country,
the glass that is not a glass but a truck filled
with bodies hemmed together by barbed wire.

A truck that yesterday was filled with toxic barrels,
and before that money, and before that money.
To you who chew with your mouths open
as I become a desert and a war zone.

To those empty spaces that exist when a man's
words become familiar ghosts. To those who spoke
of rebellion before the moon crawled on to their backs,
and now their bodies itch with maggots in a ditch.

To the palm of the immortals who raised the river from its bed
and had its waters stare a man in the eye. To the never-ending
silence that knew us before we were human. To those that thirst
and hold their hands like brackets waiting for thunder,
searching for the shape a body makes when in prayer.

EXECUTIONER'S SONG

How do I curse in my father's language
when the world and all its dangers
watch me from a bedroom window?
A crow floating in its darkness rests
on a street lamp. The garden's music
joins me – my silence a unit of space.
A shadow falls and creeps into a room.
The moon soft in its approach meets
with my mind's ghost. Raindrops gather
like mercury. On a moist hill the church
sits like a crown. Faults in the creases
of my shirt rest against my hard surface.
A broken song drifts up in the night's blindness
like cigar smoke from the back of a car.
The chorus knows that I have no home.
What if I told you my country was a French film
where every woman I have loved belongs
to a song I have sung? The subtitles
on their breasts call it the silent tide of blood.
With such reds it is best when drinking wine
to hold your breath and close your eyes like fists.
Dear body of mine, where are you from?
As the dark moves towards a body that is better
than myself, draw me a map where leaves fall,
where every song is not a song of war.

THE OLD DARK

There are men in townships
like ours who hold a rifle
as they would a woman.

Beyond this field, a valley is waiting,
as one would for the apocalypse,
for the old river, before roads led to it,
or Livingstone's maps found you, before
the mountains grew their backs,
before sight was tempered, before
the revelation on a sky's blank page.

In this perfect chalice of night
you are not the first pilgrim to ask
the oracle, *What will I become?*

Sunsets have seen this blue bend
its way around a hill towards a village
without lights, banked with marram
and bush; above a ribbon of stars,
below walls of torn-up tents.

No words govern why some men
are good according to the law,
some to the state, yet others
can lead men away from their fields,
away from the perfumes of a season
and the river's scent of tilapia.

If I could have stopped with my third tongue
the sky from stretching its arms across
the horizon, as the serpent Nile
opens its mouth towards a sea,
or watched as midnight stars blink

in a constellation, as god watches
your wife wash silk in a stream,
would I not have stopped
your country's screams?

THE GOOD LIGHT

Part of an invisible unit ambush
a refugee camp on unmarked streets.
On television a flame glows.
A slow train clicks on a far-off track
as my name is scratched on the wall
of a cell. The world is charged.
Some local newscaster tells us

Today we are tearing ourselves apart.

Those aren't the words she uses.
Watch her eyes. In this lost world
I take my cue from the city's silence.
The Nile flows quietly by.
Gunmen surround my house.

The mob gather in their greatness,
tearing doors off their hinges,
searching for permits. The hour
is about four. In the stillness
that comes before dawn, I ooze
like oil into the darkness.

Alone at last, but not intentionally
dressed as a hawker, there is a city
inside me, in a space filled
with the rest of my life.
My city is a burning flame.
There is no word for this uniform
that once belonged to someone else.

I am my father's crop breathing dark elements.
Words move the needle. Once with my own silence
I coaxed the Narus River from its bed, waiting
in the folds of a night for a moment in time.
Waiting seven years for the grandeur of God.
Waiting for the good light that brings
all things into blossom. Waiting to leave.

LEGION

Who carved a child from the shadows
and placed it in my womb, to grow in a kiln
of dark earth, from dust into dust,
from loneliness into life, my light in you?

While others waved at their windows
and called you redeemer, were my hands
not the gourd that poured water down your throat,
asking all worlds to be restored by running water?

Even a rock stays by the stream to curve its edges.
You stone, you blade, you marrow, you soil, you fever,
you wall, you light. The light of extinction, light of my word
turned milk, to music, to woodsmoke on your garments.

One memory's ignorance hides another;
it bends a man into something else – an Ancholi
a soldier, a monster, a slap of music on the skin
that dances between a raging wound and its surrender.

Wait for the rising of your body,
for a government placed in your hands,
for the walls to return to walls and the floor
once more to become the sound of you.

JED:

I am sitting at Terminal Two customs
in King Abdulaziz International Airport,
my Ugandan passport in my top left
breast pocket, holding onto an unopened
mint condition "Jetfire" Transformer
that my mum bought in East Street
market – my only companion as I wait
for my dad. Through the heatproof glass
I see white Muslims gathered for the Hajj
at the pilgrims' terminal tent shaped
with Teflon-coated skin. Jetfire says
it reminds him of Charlton Heston in
The Ten Commandments. I can't see Moses.

BLACK DEATH

Two men who have never had a country of their own
fall out over a girl in a bar. In place of war they pull off their shirts,
lunatics in an embrace, as a barmaid fills my glass with local ale.

Policemen hang out of armed cars with sophisticated weapons.
Fleas fry on their backs as a ricochet gives voice to the air.
At full stretch, a camera blinks at an unshaven male, clearly dead.

They are beating his body while I stand outside myself.
A year from now I will suffer the same death by water.
This body will be a map in the dark, moving towards a shore.

By the open stove of my wife's village there will be death by surprise,
death by marriage, death by having rummaged into the past,
into the distant past of a man that neither of us remembers.

After boycott marches there will be death by placards.
In radio silence, Israeli ground-troops will storm a home
looking for the Archbishop. Death by Judas kiss.

Lizard-coloured helicopters filled with embassy-men and snipers
with walkie-talkies will signal for death by longshot. Demonstrators
behind masks, with eyes like loaded dice, will ask for death by decay,

the body turning black, blood-let like a pig. The crowd is here
offering false compliments to an immigrant on his knees.
Death by confession – words that are not your own.

A note whispered in earshot of a *New York Times* news crew
as man sets fire to himself. The body now an animal bent double,
a shadow of vague form promising to raise itself from the earth.

THE SELF (1979)

Don't quote me, but I swear the radio hissed:
Run for your lives. Anyway! Fast forward and
I'm being taken by the hand to Entebbe Airport.

Commercial flights are cancelled. There's a queue
of people with the right faces but wrong surnames
and no luggage waiting for a cargo plane to London –

people I barely know, but they swear they know me
well. Smiles disguise thoughts that if spoken,
would get us, you know, arrested, or worse. Then,

somebody shouts, *There's space in the front*.
Under floodlights we're shuffled in, Noah's Ark-style,
travelling all night, leaving the sun behind.

Only clouds show their form, when the colour
of the sky has gone, as the engines purr in a
constant exhalation. The future is speeding towards me.

A loud darkness leaks through the cabin window.
I'm listening to it, not the noise, but the rhythm.
This high above the world, in between time,

I can't help but wonder: now that we have left
our country, who will turn out the lights?
In the terminal my ears are popping

when the immigration officer steps from his desk,
with my mother's passport in hand and asks me,
just like you did, *Tell me that story again*.

THE LAST UGANDAN

It is hard to believe that blood unites a tribe.
My country is landlocked and ruled by guerrilla forces.
Boys are kidnapped to serve as solders with guns.

Beneath the mountains of misty Ruwenzori, sugar cane,
tobacco and cotton grow; girls are routinely raped and
become sex slaves or "wives" of rebel commanders.

Sometime in the day the light or water will go.
In the paraffin-light evenings curfews begin,
the tradition inherited from past dictators.

My mother bought me a plane ticket to flee Idi Amin.
He was a powerful man, loved by many women.
Mum says she "sees" my father in him.

FATHER CORNELIUS

With three torn hundred-dollar bills, he made the last table
of six at the end of the second day. His seven-deuce offsuit
in the big blind flopped a full house, which he slow-played
against a pair of aces and red kings. This hand eliminated
the final two players for a seat in the finals at the bar.

Here's the dirt. They used to call him the Saint, learnt to
play poker close to the vest by watching Texas Slim and
Johnny Ross, who won $10,000 at Amarillo Slim's Texas
tournament in the 80s. He never chased cards, and mumbled
when the dealer tapped the table.

Saint mastered the bluff while training as a pastor in Nairobi –
"private" games for high stakes after confession. His wit and
charm took their chips, harvesting the tells in their eyes and
hands. After the river card he'd take you by the hand and pray,
Receive the Body and Blood of Christ.

Father Cornelius offered wafers and a swig of Brugal to his
travelling congregation. Always on his way to some place else,
with a pack of playing cards tucked under the belt.
Now middle-aged, his hairline receding like a low tide,
his lips mouthing a number.

Under the soft lights of Nairobi Casino, roulette tables spun
like fans in the bayou. Past the cranked levers of fruit machines,
rings of tobacco smoke left the corners of his mouth,
right hand tweaked a pile of chips, dog collar in pocket,
as he eyed the waitress through black spectacles.

In cracked stilettos she poured him a Cuban Mojito in a tall glass.
Two shots of dark rum topped up by the flask in his blazer.
Sucking on the lemon he would swirl fistfuls of fresh

mint leaves with his cigar. The flop was already on the table;
if he bet now the pot would be too shallow.

After a minute's stare, he pushed his chips in the middle and ordered
a plate of nyama choma. The crowd knew he needed the risk of looking
at the river card. Under his lifted thumb, the jack and nine of diamonds.
After swigs of Brugal, curses turned to prayers.

THE LIBERATION

Your name, which used to be another name,
cannot be used by your men or the people
that love you. You used to be a boy
throwing pebbles at the machine
before the switch went off in your head,
or was it behind the shirt? The truth of this place
will always be the same. Remember this night
as if it were another day. Do not be afraid of it.
It will bear its name with the shallow moon
that gives you its eyes to watch the darkness
crumble away, as if there were another night.

Watch how it reveals a clock tower
of sleepy soldiers, and to its left Lake Victoria
slapping water against the shore. Now ask yourself
about the four planes kite-landing on the road,
your commandos on their bellies, how you moved
like smoke across the red dirt towards the second
terminal, fanning out as you would for a deity
around Entebbe airport, your women and children
squatting in a room of exposed wires, walls peeling.
No man asks for war. It is a costume one wears
when the earth erupts, before a political sign,
before the sign of money, before your fisted
command, before the silence, before the scent
of petrol, before the liberation of ghosts.

THE SHEPHERD

At the violet hour, when the eyes and back
Turn upward from the desk, when the human engine waits
Like a taxi throbbing waiting. — T.S. Eliot, *The Wasteland*

Made no appeal. Spoke only of an assassination plot
at the diplomats' independence party. Caught whispers
among the bushes. Four men making finger-maps in the dirt.
Dressed in violet house-boy attire. Can you believe that at this hour?

Continue! Height: tall. Complexion: pallid, body hairs sheared.
When asked, he mimicked how each stood in formation.
The only time they relaxed was in the drawing of guns.
In the eyes an expansion.

Continue! They were ready to die and watch the world burn
with them. Questioned for hours on his back, his right cheek
on the tarmac of a dual carriageway, a turn of the neck to watch
the stars with his flock, their gaze upwards interrupted by a blast

of diesel and cough of smoke from the right.
A base hum tickling his shoulders rises through the road.
Two Coco-Cola soda crates were used as a makeshift desk to the left.

Continue! The voice from behind asked and when the only answer
was a sigh (a meter was running) into the evening, the voice took
a blade. You'll always find a use for it. Humans are pathetic!

Continue! The voice asks another to dig some graves.
Engine off. This was not the shepherd's war, yet he waits
and offers his body to those who beat him, their faces and hands
like flint. In the first grave his feet, now just cuts of meat.
A second grave, his arms dying like the rusty flowers by the taxi.
In the third and fourth, his cracked skull and torso throbbing.
The goats, searching for a command, graze at his graves.

BIRD IN FLAMES

A man and his beer talks to another man; after a swig from a dark
bottle his lips leak out a *Hmmm*. In the first death I am a bird
darting from an oncoming pick-up truck under starlight, as I head
for the grass. A static quiet. The pick-up drives down the road.
Two men mention genocide, a third struggles to confess that he
has spoken to the tribes and it stirred conflict.

Earlier, the third man was blindfolded, a hand resting at the
bottleneck of his throat, a knife at his wrists. Others surrounded
him in a circle under a low purple light. Discomfort dripped from
his mouth. They were looking for a reaction. The moment was
disguised as a get-together, hence the beer, meat and chapattis
and women's voices outside rising over music.

The third man's arms are crossed as a deep voice enters the
discussion and asks him, *Truthfully, Bishop, where are the arms*? The
night has an Indian heat; silence glues the third man to his seat.
The Voice has set a table. He leans into the bishop's ear, rolls his
sleeve and invites him to join, once he has told them where the
guns are. *The guns! The guns.*

The bishop replies, *I can live without your formality, without these
courtesies. What meal have you prepared that I have not eaten?* The
Voice kicks his chair out from under him. Back in the pick-up the
bodies are not moving; no side glances. They pass a school, a
settlement, a store, a trading post in the hills, but there is no
conversation.

Notice the bird. The car's headlights are like fireflies. Since the
moment has passed I can tell you there was no bird, but the men
were real, and the table full of food. The only things missing are
the bullets. A second death. That is how nations die over there.
When I say nation I mean tribe, when I say tribe I mean people,
when I say over there I mean here.

WE THE JANUARY

We the January, talk to you who lived inside us,
who from our hillsides and escarpments
have moved our livestock and crops
despite our ancestral claims.

You who burned the thatched tombs
of our kings to dust, lighting the night like a candle,
leaving villagers looking for words
when mud walls crumbled to crust,

you have never had to live like your body
was always on fire, to know the death
of your body and still remain in it.
It is a shield this language of darkness —

its movements, its clothing, its marked
shapelessness. It reflects lake and shore,
it moves like the folds of my heart.
There are no soft sounds for this purchase.

My voice is a foreigner testing the air of my own homestead.
But a man can only go halfway trying to climb back
into his own daylight before the mirage of his past
cuts through a field like flame fingers reaping a cotton harvest.

HOW TO PAINT A WAR

Three things feel useful to me:
my father's voice, the flame of it,
black smoke rising over a fallen sun.
His last slow breath saw one body
drag another up a street looking for smokes
in the breast pocket of the dead.

I have his wallet, but no lighter.
I know his face, but after ten minutes
of watching this sleep you count yourself lucky
that you can say your name out loud
and that you are not him wrapped around bone
like old muscle on the street outside.

Without the stool there is no king,
no throne. Tribesmen worship
clumps of human hair.
The creek we used to leap barefoot into
is a pan where the body's yolk is split.
Roads turn into snakes.

This is what passes for nightlife.
After curfew, stealing your fingers
across a woman's thigh means, *Why not?*
On the radio, a translator uses
static silence to describe paramilitaries
lining up newsmen for execution.

Headshot, close range. Dried vermillion
blood like Rorschach blots tattooed
on the wall of millet factory.
Blame the inspector general,
those with locomotives eyes
who did it for God and country.

DEATHFALL

Before Koni, before Museveni, before Obote's second term,
before now there was me. We were in deep shit! Bridges couldn't be fixed
with gaffer-tape. America stopped lending plasticine to fill pot-holes.
I quit playing refugee. Who among you was going to pay our country's
light bill? Well? You uninvited guests like Rome, you will know where
we put the bodies in their tunics and kangas, my sins, both real and imagined,
into the trap. To my brother, my rival, when he comes, don't let him tap
the glass, idiots, devise his death. You stable-god, a month's worth
of grain for the paratroop regiment won't purge you.

New wives and shoes and a move to State House while we live in huts.
Home will see your troubles cursed. By the way, your Chief of Police:
into the trap! You who believed in Churchill's prophecy. You innocents
ruled by a spinning earth, your tears will quench the barns we set fire to.
You who call your guns She. You papier mâché martyrs
with north Kiboko accents. You shadow soldiers who dig dead men
from their graves. You in the motion of battle. You who search the airwaves
for the British World Service, who stare spirits in the face
but can't stand heights, the rules say: into the trap.

I will not forgive the clan who sheds blood for party politics.
Your god might. The one with his hands up as he waves, ask the firing squad
to send him with the widowers, orphans and motherless sons, into the trap.
All you disciples of empires. Mr Men ministers who paraphrase over
PA systems: into the trap. Wrecked after five days of being held
under decree nineteen. Why riffle through your Yellow pages in search
of Heads-of-state? Into the trap. The executioner who lets you watch
his navel after bare-knuckle fights: into the trap. You who played
The Bard on screen and stage, or quoted Aristotle: into the trap.

Your second tongue: into the trap. Lumino-boy with that Yankee
dialect: into the trap. It makes no difference to me, you sun worshipper.
Name your Icarus and fly into the trap. You who abandon
your wife's thighs for the cradle of a servant girl: into the trap.

You at The Uganda Company Limited (Trojans), because you gave us
cotton but took our land, follow me with your horse mask,
into the trap. Those who offer me your skins as a fig leaf, let me carve
a map on your backs to Ithaca. You can hitchhike for all I care:
into the trap. Take your stand with the soothsayer in her snake dress.
The ones who hesitate: into the trap.

\

CDG:

Sad is the man who is asked for a story
and can't come up with one. It is not that I have difficulty
with endings, I have lost where I began. When my eyes fall
like curtains to untie this portion of the evening,
a splinter is removed from my palm and I am a boy again.
Death leans against my face to pose a question,
a blade that undresses the skin to leave me flayed,
unshapen, iridescent flame. Later, while lying awake,
my tongue will search for a song. What you hear is true.
The chorus knows that I have no home.
Shaded walls can't guard me. Shadows cannot hide.
I pierce the valance of the wind and on its breath I glide.
No soil is sacred. I have no country to call a church.

THE RETURN

God, bent in time,
repeats himself — César Vallejo

How will you know me
in the city I call home,
in which I am a guest?

You will not find me
in the womb. My birth
is a bruise healed.

This evening in the silence
I rose from my humiliation.
With brittle nails and torn garments

I fell to the floor, palms
facing down. Shame and disgrace
weighed on my head.

I did not know where
to put my eyes. In forgetting you
and my country, my transgressions

are larger than me. When the guilt
reached my heart, I spoke to you!
I am one of those children

of Ugandan progeny who fled.
Cloaked in night, I left my kings and clans
in captivity, their blood and land

at the mercy of the rifle.
Today, foreign chiefs use our machetes
and lust for blood to rule us.

SMOKE

When the mountains stared at our backs,
it was my mother who read the sky, its cobalt
glass full of moisture. The clouds formed

a necklace at the summit. If I could remember
the smell I would describe this as well – though
I do recall the smoke trying to join with the clouds,

each tendril plume learning to fly. These birds
of smoke released themselves from the dung
hut-chimney as my body rested on her back.

Braced in the sling of her shawl she sang
in a language I no longer recognise
but can identify from sound. Like water.

FROM THE KING

Do no work today, cousins, we are marked to die.
Feast with your neighbour, then we will depart.

Take care of your tongue, watch what the lips say,
for foreign words uprooted our pumpkins.

Let us not inherit the stupidity of our forefathers
who, like dust, abandoned their homestead.

Smear your bodies in red oil. Tonight we split the darkness.
We will be remembered as the wild cats

who smeared their bodies in blood. The fewer our men,
the greater our share of honour. Do not count your coins;

there is nothing you need from gold. Our bodies will be
our wealth. Even the grave will not reject our clansmen.

It's Uganda's loss if we live. Curse the man who does not
share this fellowship and fears our desires. He is mucus

in the mouth, a rotting fruit. He was not carved out of the rock
as we were. Find the stomach to fight.

Let courage be your host. Shed your blood with me, brothers.
When they name this day, you who live will show your scars.

Wear them as you would the kikoys in your hut.
Hold vigil. You who see old age, tell this to your sons.

Let us be the throb in our children's dreams
and the wounds they wear under their skins.

THE UNION

Yesterday in Kampala there's a queue
from Independence Park to Mulago hospital.

A sign reads "Mercenaries on Strike". Waiting
out a war more like. Story goes a houseboy

on his bike was stopped at an intersection.
He must have been doing thirty easy.

He chucks my contraband in the banana grove.
The Lieutenant beckons him to stop as he does the rounds.

A stick of bubble gum bobs in and out of his mouth.
The scratchy radio broadcasts tells him that the Romans –

code word for rebels – are gathering by the Empire
(you guessed it – Lake Victoria). Empty out your pockets.

Once. The boy keeps chewing. Twice. He sweats the world.
Ospreys have departed from the scene. On three, a gum-balloon

the size of a speech-bubble pops. A bullet to the back of the head.
Dead with identity cards in hand. The doctor-man who made a joke,

the bank clerk who gave the houseboy the gum, the mzungu
from the World Service and his camera man, and the bartender

who gave the soldiers a tab – at least they weren't buried alive
in the forest south of the Coca-Cola bottling factory, fingernails

full of dirt, unglued. Bullets sent from the trees make little noise.
The boy is left to bleed into the street.

The Lieutenant's men are waiting in the wings; they are sick
of the bodies, propped up and burned in cars, jamming up market stalls,

clogging rivers, stinking airport runways, taking up newborns'
space on mothers' backs. How are you supposed to enjoy

an African fairytale when all the exiles are gone?
We are being exploited. Someone should set up a union.

THRONE OF WEAPONS:

In your other world you are song;
in this one you are a gun.
By the anthill a young boy fishes
for tilapia in the woods; another
is transforming arms into tools
by the church. The stone altar rests
on damp earth with stale wine
in the sunlight, a good light.
Jesus is emerging from a tomb
telling stories in the language
of my father in the courtyard.
The gravel of his voice rises
an octave. I am looking for one way
to become another when the field
behind me blooms. My eyes
become cameras. I am stone
and flint shaped like a man.
To say I exist is the bullseye
in the middle of the Galaxy.
Planets make us what we are,
a tribe that has forgotten
everything it has outlived.

TRAVELLER

Barefoot I push a bicycle to a new village, entering with a song to hide this face's signature. Through a glass darkly the heart stops, dead weight. I am leaning by a fence afraid, not of shadows — they are nobody's fault — but of time, the unseen persistence. The mob form a circle around me and I wonder do fish pay any mind to rain. I wish I could be two elements! At the intersection I am older by two minutes. Watchmen carved from camphor arrest a man with my face without ID and pull up his trouser legs. Inked calluses show where army boots had been. Gunshots from the wood disrupt the hour. I shouldn't have lied about the rifle-strap marks. They search for my tax card and jest: *Your graveyard the river can be seen from space.*

ELECTRIC DEAD

A fire's tail cuts through a field, flamed fingers
reaping the cotton harvest, baptised by God's thick
kerosene breath. The enemy is a sea of fire,
so the TV camera tells me. Even when a slick

reporter untangles a black microphone wire to
reword the status quo. God holds the balance
in this uncertain hour. A crimson night cuts through
an open sky. My skin weeps stars in their ascension dance.

The beauty of this land cannot be contained in a lifetime.
But there are those with the innocent wish to find a way out
of their own bodies. There is only so much playing dead a mind
can take before it finds a road, river or window to climb through.

There are men who are Lazarus whose fates are made certain
by the addition of disaster. Death is its own attraction.
To look at eternity and not return. To escape your own bloodstain.
The photograph knows your form living in two worlds without division.

Find an event with no photograph, a story carried in the mouths
of others, a memory in which I too am the observer looking
for a passage of light, searching for a border or coastline, south
of something that I can call new. Is it found in the weight of the heart

the darkness reaches out to me? Calling me by name,
"Love is a burning tree", you are its sovereign flame?
Bodies grow out of the ground surrounded by policemen.
Some in uniform, some with rifles, some not. Vultures the lot of them.

THE GATE

The last I remember there were three of us
running, travelling through ochre dust following
fireflies as long as the path decided.

If we had stayed in our village we would have become
lives carved open. Would you believe I used to play
hide-and-seek in these woods, by the high grass,

using the night rains as cover? The road's shoulder
was a marker. Lorries would bully their way over
the tarmac. Their headlamps were corridors of light

that you could use to pick up speed. The earth
would take your weight if you danced along it.
There is a way of leaning into an evening's camber

with all your momentum that turns you and the world
into one. If you ask, the river will hold your breath
in a covenant of silence. My brother used to wonder

how I disappeared after his ten count. With one palm
in front of the other, like a drunk sleepwalker,
he would push himself into the night to look for me.

DRIVE-IN

Plot:

> *The chessboard is the world, the pieces are the phenomena of the*
> *Universe, the rules of the game are what we call the laws of Nature*
> *and the player on the other side is hidden from us"* — Thomas Huxley

Scene:
In the Datsun we follow Thika road to its natural end.
Where it curves, cars trail behind us in a wagon train.
The earth grinds to black butter under the tyres.

I am the voyeur trying to fit the images to the frame.
The name of the film is gone, but Roger Moore is Bond.
A comet of light-rays moves towards the screen.

In this tail of celestial dust dragonflies float in the inertia.
My eyes obediently follow the credits,
a dark watermark of words against a canvas altar.

Outside, the moon expands as rain drips off the trees.
Beyond the verandah a familiar sky hangs in the air.
These visions are a river of time and memory.

CITIZEN…

what if without saying a thing,
this one-way ticket to Heathrow
gets us past immigration, through
metal detectors and the x-ray machine,

down escalators to baggage-handling
and the armed guards following us
on security cameras. What then? As
I sit on a leather chair, watching

our reflections copy us, copying
the man with the FHM magazine
turn the page. My language

cannot ask him the time. Since we landed
I am two hours behind. A heartbeat caught
in my throat. Can't return to the country I know.
The airport is my changing room.

If this country fits just right,
if we can survive the night,
I might live here for the rest of our lives.

LHR:

An airport is a room. I keep talking
as if my body is elsewhere. In full sight
of a crimson God, as children we were burdens,
coffins with eyes. A professor steps into the light
to educate us. *You can't kill the dead twice.*
Has he seen the militia slide down a mountain like goats,
or a beating heart explode onto a barrack wall?
Even the coffee I brought back in hand luggage
when poured in a cup is an eye, a past dark,
itching for light. So, since I cannot be the memory
of your death, let me bend the way a river does,
all shadow and sound, around a hill, towards a village
I once recognised. There are days
when this unplanned landscape speaks its music.

BIOGRAPHICAL NOTE

Nick Makoha is a Cave Canem Graduate Fellow and Complete Works Alumni who represented Uganda at Poetry Parnassus as part of the Cultural Olympiad held in London. A former Writer in Residence for Newham Libraries, his one-man show *My Father & Other Superheroes* debuted to sold-out performances at 2013 London Literature Festival and is currently on tour. In 2005 award-winning publisher Flipped-eye launched its pamphlet series with his debut *The Lost Collection of an Invisible Man*. Part of *The Kingdom of Gravity* is in the anthology *Seven New Generation African Poets* (Slapering Hol Press). He is the 2016 winner of the Toi Derricotte & Cornelius Eady Chapbook Prize for his manuscript "Resurrection Man", to be published by Jai-Alai Books in spring 2017. He won the 2015 Brunel International African Poetry prize and his poems have appeared in *Poetry Review*, *Rialto*, *The Triquarterly Review*, *Boston Review*, *Callaloo*, and *Wasafiri*. He is a Creative Entre-preneur-in-Residence at Goldsmiths, working to create an in-depth online digital archive of the metic experiences of Black British Writers. Find him at www.nickmakoha.com

THANKS:

To the families and communities and tribes that I belong to. This book was made possible because you made space for me to write, think, learn and be. I cannot name all of you so let me nominate a few to represent the whole; Ngugi wa Thiong'o, Terrance Hayes, Rita Dove, Toi Derricotte, Cornelius Eady, Malika Booker, Chris Abani, Robin Coste Lewis, Kwame Dawes, Bernardine Evaristo, George Szirtes, Roger Robinson, Morgan Parker, Margo Stever, Judith Palmer, Scott Cunningham, Eva Salzman, Dante Micheaux, Mimi Khalvati, Zakia Henderson-Brown, Patricia Smith, Evie Shockley, Nicole Sealey, Mahogany L. Browne, John Murillo, Nii Parkes, Gregory Pardlo, Danez Smith, Dr Nathalie Teitler, Maura Dooley, Professor Joan Anim-Addo, Inua Ellams, Warsan Shire, Safia Elhillo, Peter Kahn, Langston Kerman, Caleb Femi, Willie Perdomo, Stephen Knight and Jack Underwood.

Thanks also to the following institutions, without which I would not have had the resources to complete this work: Goldsmiths MA programme; Alumni, Cave Canem Foundation; The Complete Works; Malika's Kitchen; Callaloo; Spread the Word; Arvon; Apples & Snakes; Renaissance One; Arts Council England; British Council; The Society Of Authors; Creative Works London; RundemCrew; Southbank Centre; Speaking Volumes; Africa Writes; The Poetry Society; The Poetry Foundation; The Poetry School; Hudson Valley Writers Centre and the Royal African Society.